MW00535223

Cutting Edge Careers in
SCIENCE

Don Nardo

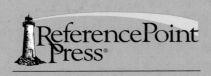

ReferencePoint
Press®

San Diego, CA

About the Author

Classical historian, amateur astronomer, and award-winning author Don Nardo has written numerous volumes about scientific topics, including *Destined for Space* (winner of the Eugene M. Emme Award for best astronomical literature); *Tycho Brahe*, winner of the National Science Teacher's Association's best book of the year; *Planet Under Siege*; *Climate Change*; *Deadliest Dinosaurs*; and *The History of Science*. Nardo, who also composes and arranges orchestral music, lives with his wife Christine in Massachusetts.

For more information, contact:
ReferencePoint Press, Inc.
PO Box 27779
San Diego, CA 92198
www.ReferencePointPress.com

Picture Crtedits:

Cover: Likoper/Shutterstock.com
 6: Maury Aaseng
20: wavebreakmedia/Shutterstock.com
35: Jevtic/Shutterstock.com
50: Evgeny Haritonov/Shutterstock.com
59: Monkey Business Images/Shutterstock.com
66: FrameStockFootages/Shutterstock.com

LIBRARY OF CONGRESS CATALOGING-IN-PUBLICATION DATA

Names: Nardo, Don, 1947- author.
Title: Cutting edge careers in science / by Don Nardo.
Description: San Diego, CA : ReferencePoint Press, 2021. | Series: Cutting edge STEM careers | Includes bibliographical references and index.
Identifiers: LCCN 2020003697 (print) | LCCN 2020003698 (ebook) | ISBN 9781682828755 (library binding) | ISBN 9781682828762 (ebook)
Subjects: LCSH: Science--Vocational guidance--Juvenile literature.
Classification: LCC Q147 .N28 2021 (print) | LCC Q147 (ebook) | DDC 502.3--dc23
LC record available at https://lccn.loc.gov/2020003697
LC ebook record available at https://lccn.loc.gov/2020003698

Contents

Why Become a Scientist?

In April 2019, Russian biochemists at the Peoples' Friendship University (RUDN) in Moscow isolated a chemical that is produced in the human body and acts to slow down the death of cells. Cell damage and death naturally increase as people age, and one reason people manage to live as long as they do, the researchers showed, is that that particular chemical slows down the aging process to some degree. The biochemists who isolated the chemical are hopeful that finding ways to manipulate it may eventually lead to the ability to prolong human lifetimes.

A few months later, in September 2019, astronomers at University College in London announced the results of a study they had been working on for several months. Using the orbiting Hubble Space Telescope and other advanced devices, they found water vapor in the atmosphere of an Earth-like planet in a star system lying hundreds of trillions of miles away. Among the thousands of extrasolar planets (those in alien star systems) discovered in the past two decades, several are Earth-sized. Also, most have atmospheres. But until this discovery, no one had confirmed the presence of water on any of those faraway worlds. The University College researchers demonstrated that the conditions for Earth-like life exist throughout the universe.

These important findings, only two of dozens that expanded the frontiers of human knowledge in 2019 alone, were the result of the vision, persistence, and hard work of scientists. Scientific learning has been part of many ancient cultures. In the Western world, the first scientists emerged in Greece more than twenty-five centuries ago. They established a handful of scientific disciplines—notably astronomy, medicine, biology, botany, and mechanics. The march of science ensued, slowly at first, but with astounding speed in the past two centuries. During that mere wink of an eye in historical terms, science quite literally transformed the world. It revolutionized the way people dress, eat, learn, communicate, work, travel, fight disease, play, and make war. Today more than two hundred separate scientific disciplines exist, and thousands of colleges and other schools regularly train new scientists to maintain and operate those disciplines.

To Make a Difference

The young people who decide to make science their career have numerous other potential professions to choose from, of course. They can, if they want, go into business or finance; the law and law enforcement; agriculture and food production; writing and other literary fields; the arts and entertainment; politics and public service; and many others. Why, then, do some choose to devote their lives to science?

When pressed to answer that question, many scientists answer roughly the same way as Jason Todd, a lab technician at Polymer Solutions, an independent testing laboratory in Virginia. "You can really make a difference in the world," he says. "All the technological and medical advancements that improve our quality of life are based on discoveries made by scientists."[1] One of Todd's coworkers, Olivia Brescia, agrees. "Science is behind almost every convenience in life," she remarks. "People never stop to ask questions like, why is the water I drink safe to use? Or, how does this liquid cough syrup cure my head cold symptoms?"[2]

In addition to providing most of the common conveniences of everyday life, scientific research and development have repeatedly solved global challenges and problems, benefiting humanity as a whole. "We live in a technological world," says Dick Ahlstrom, science editor of the *Irish Times*. "And its complexity continues to throw up challenges that require answers. Some are life and death, for example finding new energy sources that can reduce the damage caused by climate change. And then there is world hunger: how can you get innovations in agriculture out into the field in poorer parts of the world so that people have enough to eat?"[3]

Attributes That Matter to Employers

Written communication skills and the ability to solve problems are at the top of the list of attributes employers look for when considering new hires. This is the finding of a report titled "Job Outlook 2019." The report comes from the National Association of Colleges and Employers (NACE), an organization that surveys employers nationwide to learn more about their hiring plans in connection with recent college graduates. Other desirable attributes include the ability to work in a team setting, showing initiative, analytical skills, and a strong work ethic.

Attribute	% of Respondents
Communication skills (written)	82.0%
Problem-solving skills	80.9%
Ability to work in a team	78.7%
Initiative	74.2%
Analytical/quantitative skills	71.9%
Strong work ethic	70.8%
Communication skills (verbal)	67.4%
Leadership	67.4%
Detail oriented	59.6%
Technical skills	59.6%
Flexibility/adaptability	58.4%
Computer skills	55.1%
Interpersonal skills (relates well to others)	52.8%
Organizational ability	43.8%
Strategic planning skills	38.2%
Tactfulness	25.8%
Creativity	23.6%
Friendly/outgoing personality	22.5%
Entrepreneurial skills/risk-taker	16.9%
Fluency in a foreign language	11.2%

Source: "Job Outlook 2019," NACE, November 2018.
www.odu.edu/content/dam/odu/offices/cmc/docs/nace/2019-nace-job-outlook-survey.pdf.

Ahlstrom's mention of climate change is a dramatic example of the need for many more trained, dedicated, reliable scientists. Overwhelming evidence gathered by climate scientists in the last three decades shows conclusively that the planet's atmosphere is warming at an increasing rate and that this trend will lead to rising sea levels, extreme weather events, and other catastrophic consequences. "The climate has always changed," explains Mark Serreze, director of the National Snow and Ice Data Center, in Boulder, Colorado. "But we're seeing now rapid change, very quick, and that's the thing that species have a hard time adapting to."[4] To significantly slow the onslaught of climate change, he adds, will require a better understanding of how it works, and a great many more devoted, hard-working climate scientists will be needed.

Curiosity and Fascination

The desire to become a scientist can arise from a smaller-scale, more personal level as well. Asked to give advice to young people about choosing a career, many scientists point out that simple feelings such as curiosity and fascination can be key. Finding various elements of the natural world compelling or enchanting might lead to a lucrative career. One vocal advocate of this pathway is University of Delaware astronomer Harry Shipman, who recalls, "When I was eight years old, I looked up at the sky and wondered what the stars were made of. Later, I picked up rocks, admired them and the landscapes which they made, and wondered how it all came to be. . . . All aspects of the natural world fascinate me. I was lucky to have found a way to get paid for doing what I like so much."[5]

Climate Scientist

A Few Facts

Number of Jobs
About 10,000

Pay
An average of $94,000 per year

Educational Requirements
Minimum of a bachelor's degree

Personal Qualities
Strong math and computer skills, attention to detail, burning curiosity about how the world works

Work Settings
Mostly labs and offices; less often outside field work

Future Job Outlook
Estimated growth of 8 percent through 2028

What Does a Climate Scientist Do?

Climate scientists, also called climatologists and atmospheric scientists, study the weather and climate and attempt to explain how they affect the planet and humanity. Climate scientists are quick to point out that weather and climate are often assumed by nonscientists to be synonymous, but they are actually two very different things. (*Weather* consists of the rapidly changing local atmospheric conditions in a given region; in contrast, *climate* is the normally *un*changing condition of the planet's overall atmosphere.)

To better understand both weather and climate, climate scientists employ various mechanical and digital devices. These include barometers (which measure air pressure), anemometers (wind speed), weather balloons, radar systems, and orbiting satellites equipped with state-of-the-art cameras. They also use advanced computer programs that sort through enormous amounts of data and from it make short- and long-term climate forecasts. The programs in question are extremely sophisticated and rely on highly complex mathematical models; these allow climate scientists to estimate with a fair amount of accuracy how the climate will change over the course of years and decades. Such forecasts are vital to government planners; architects and builders planning to erect new structures; companies that design heating and cooling systems; farmers and others involved in agricultural production; and military strategists.

The job of a climate scientist is both complex and diverse, in large part because it combines knowledge and training from many separate sciences. As National Aeronautics and Space Administration (NASA) climate scientist Gavin Schmidt puts it,

> Up until 20 years ago, no one was a climate scientist— people were just meteorologists, oceanographers, ecologists, geologists, or biologists, or chemists. The reason why there are now climate scientists is that we realized these things are all coupled. What happens in the ocean is not independent of what's happening with the weather, not independent of what's happening in forests.[6]

A Typical Workday

On an average workday a climate scientist deals in various ways with collected data about the workings of Earth's atmosphere, oceans, and land masses. This entails extensive use of a computer to compare present-day data with data from prior months or years, create complex computer models, exchange emails with other scientists, and write research papers, grant proposals, and articles for scientific journals. If the climate scientist is a faculty member of a college or university, a typical day might also involve teaching one or more classes.

Education and Training

Most often, climate scientists are required to have a minimum of a bachelor's (or four-year) degree. This degree can be in atmospheric science or some other scientific discipline that includes the study of the planet's atmosphere and its interaction with the oceans and land masses. For example, some climate scientists have bachelor's degrees in geology, physics, chemistry, or meteorology.

Climate scientists must have advanced course work in physics, mathematics, and meteorology, which are the bases for serious atmospheric studies. Also important are classes in computer programming and computer modeling. These are necessary because a prospective climate scientist will be expected to know how to both write and edit computer software programs that create weather and climate forecasts.

Although a bachelor's degree in these specific studies is the minimum a climate scientist will need, in most cases it will be only enough to get him or her a job as an assistant to senior scientists or managers in professional research facilities. To aim higher, the person will need both experience and more schooling. Senior scientists and managers generally must acquire at least a master's degree, and a PhD is preferable in some research institutions. These master's and PhD programs are most often in environmental science, physics, oceanography, math, statistics, meteorology, or computer science.

Skills and Personality

In order to be successful in tackling the complex and formidable challenges of their profession, climate scientists need to acquire an impressive array of scientific skills. High on the list is considerable competence in advanced math. This is because numbers, percentages, fractions, and other mathematical concepts lie at the heart of most of the tasks the job entails. Climate scientists will be constantly aided by computers, so substantial knowledge of computers and the latest climate-related computer software is also a must. In addition, robust general knowledge from a wide variety of sciences is essential to doing a credible job in climate science. These disciplines include geography, physics, geology, oceanography, and, if possible, chemistry.

Tools for Climate Science

"My primary tools for research are computer models of ecosystems. So maybe I'll be delving into the computer code to adapt the model to perform some new experiment. This process is usually about 30% writing new code, and 70% searching for the errors you've just introduced! The model then takes between a few hours and several days to run, depending on what I've asked it to do."

—Tom Pugh, climate scientist

Quoted in Embrace, "Life as a Climate Scientist." www.embrace-project.eu.

Personal skills and certain positive personality traits are also important to a successful climate scientist. First, no one in the profession works alone. Rather, the typical climate scientist is part of a team that takes on or is assigned the task of solving certain climate-related mysteries. Thus, the ability to work well with others is crucial. Also, members of the profession need to be detail oriented and very thorough, as missing a single detail can mean losing a vital clue to solving the puzzle at hand.

Another major facet of an effective climate scientist's personality is a deep-seated curiosity about the world and especially about how the planet's atmosphere works. Climate scientist Daniel Swain explains,

I've always been fascinated by the atmosphere. I grew up watching clouds and reading weather maps. As an undergraduate studying atmospheric science, it became apparent to me that despite our solid understanding regarding the "big picture" surrounding global warming, there was still quite a bit of uncertainty surrounding the details. How is regional climate changing, and how does global warming affect extreme weather? It seemed to me that the answers to these kinds of questions are critical in making practical adaptations in a warming world.[7]

Driven by Religious Faith

"[Climate change is] a humanitarian issue. It disproportionately affects the poorest and most vulnerable people here in the U.S. as well as around the world. So I thought to myself, how can I—who believes that we are to love others as we've been loved ourselves by God—how can I not do everything I can to give people who do not have a voice the voice they need to help us fix this problem."

—Katharine Hayhoe, climate scientist

Quoted in CBS News, "To Fight Climate Change, First 'Talk About It,' Climate Scientist Says," February 27, 2019. www.cbsnews.com.

Oceanographer and climate scientist Mike Williams agrees about the importance of the curiosity factor for anyone who might consider doing what he does. "I think the thing I like most about doing scientific research is the problem solving," he says. "It's not so much that I want to know everything there is about icebergs or sea ice. I want to find out why we don't know things about icebergs or sea ice."[8]

Working Conditions

Although most climate scientists spend the bulk of their working hours in indoor settings—including offices, labs, and weather stations—they also sometimes do field work outdoors. This may including checking or replacing weather equipment set up on mountaintops or in forests, deserts, and so forth; doing follow-up work on extreme weather events in different sectors of the world; and investigating all sorts of atmospheric and oceanographic phenomena in a wide range of locales.

Such field work can be tiring, fascinating, physically dangerous, exotic and romantic, or all of these things, says journalist and science writer Autumn Spanne:

Work might involve a cramped nook onboard a tiny, wave-tossed research boat navigating stormy seas, or a sweaty, mosquito-besieged tent in the middle of the rainforest. The "commute" could necessitate a snowmobile, bush plane, or a mule. Researchers must survive hungry polar bears, storms at sea, venomous snakes, and, increasingly, treacherously thin ice.[9]

Employers and Pay

According to the US Bureau of Labor Statistics (BLS), the largest single hirer of climate scientists is the federal government, which employs a little more than 30 percent of them. They typically work for agencies like the National Oceanographic and Atmospheric Administration, NASA, and various branches of the military. About 16 percent of climate scientists work for private scientific research companies; roughly 13 percent are professors at colleges and universities; and almost 10 percent work in the weather departments of television networks and stations. The rest work independently when and where they can find work.

BLS data shows that most members of this profession are well paid. The average yearly wage for a full-time climate scientist was a little over $94,000 in 2019. That means that roughly half of them earned more than that amount and the other half made less. The lowest 10 percent made a bit less than $50,000, and the highest 10 percent made just over $143,000.

What Is the Future Outlook for Climate Scientists?

The need for climate scientists is expected to increase by at least 8 percent through 2028, which is more rapid growth than the expected 7 percent average for all occupations. Indeed, all climate scientists agree that there will be increasing need for more members of their profession in the decades ahead. This, they say, is because the already large global changes in climate and weather patterns will steadily become more massive. Respected climate scientist Wolfgang Knorr explains: "The scientific data points to the fact that some catastrophic climate change is inevitable. We have already altered the climate system to a degree that is unprecedented for the last 100s of thousands of years, and the more susceptible parts of the climate system will very likely be affected, with consequences that will be catastrophic."[10]

According to Knorr and other climate scientists, as alarmed populations call on their governments to counter these adverse changes, the job of climate scientist will be in enormous demand. Daniel Swain agrees. Climate science is "a critically important endeavor," he says. "There is a real need for practicing scientists to engage with the wider world. Actively connecting with decision makers, journalists, and the public will be key in building a resilient society in the face of rapid environmental change."[11]

Find Out More

American Meteorological Society (AMS)
www.ametsoc.org

The AMS website offers information on how climate change causes extreme weather events. For aspiring climate scientists, the site explains educational pathways to becoming a climate scientist or meteorologist and how to find scholarships to study these subjects in colleges around the country.

Intergovernmental Panel on Climate Change (IPCC)
www.ipcc.ch

On the IPCC website, visitors can find the latest reports on the changing climate. They can also find information on obtaining scholarships to study climate change and how young people interested in a career in that field can write papers and reports on their own.

National Center for Atmospheric Research (NCAR)
https://ncar.ucar.edu

The website contains valuable information on college undergraduate and graduate programs that teach climate change. Also included are lists of ongoing career opportunities in the field of climate change.

National Weather Service (NWS)
www.nws.noaa.gov

The NWS website features information on how to become a meteorologist or climate scientist as well as lists of job vacancies around the country. The site also explains how students can become involved in work-study programs in these fields.

Biochemist

What Does a Biochemist Do?

Biochemistry is the study of living things at the cellular and molecular levels, and biochemists study human, animal, and plant life at those levels in an effort to understand how they work. They also seek to understand how various substances and chemicals affect human and animal tissue, how various genes or environmental factors cause disease, and how to modify crops and other plants so that they are more resistant to pests and drought. Also, some biochemists work on the development of more efficient biofuels in order to create new, clean energy sources.

No matter which particular sub-discipline or project they may be working on, at one time or another most biochemists deal with similar scientific practices and chemical substances. These include isolating certain enzymes, hormones, drugs, and toxins and analyzing their effects on the human body. In addition, virtually all biochemists employ advanced computer software to study the three-dimensional structure of molecules and use math to define the chemical relationships among various substances in nature. Finally, it is routine for biochemists to share their discoveries through writing reports and

A Few Facts

Number of Jobs
About 31,500 in 2019

Pay
An average of $93,000 per year

Educational Requirements
PhD in biochemistry, biology, or chemistry

Personal Qualities
Intense curiosity, strong attention to detail, and problem-solving skills

Work Settings
Mostly laboratories and lecture halls

Future Job Outlook
Estimated 11 percent growth through 2026

scientific articles or by lecturing in college classes or scientific conferences.

Because biochemistry explains how diverse substances affect the human body, the field plays a major role in public health. Indeed, biochemists frequently try to find the causes of various diseases, an effort which helps doctors more effectively treat sick patients. University of Glasgow biochemist Janusz Knepil summarizes this important aspect of the profession, saying that its members "use chemistry every hour of every day to investigate, diagnose and manage disease in people. There is not one person [who] has not depended on our skills for their life or health at some time."[12]

A Typical Workday

Biochemists' daily routines can vary, depending on their specialty and the particular industry or setting in which they work. Those biochemists who work in the food, brewing, and pharmaceutical industries typically spend most of their time developing new products. Among their daily duties are doing experiments in on-site labs; monitoring the manufacture of whatever items they are producing; doing quality control, either via computers or direct physical inspection; and making sure that the items are safe for ordinary people to use.

In contrast, clinical biochemists—those who work in hospitals, clinics, and medical research labs—spend the better part of a workday testing human blood as part of an effort to pinpoint the causes of a specific disease. They may also spend many hours finding and testing new treatments, sometimes directly on patients in a hospital setting.

Meanwhile, biochemists who study agriculture and the environment spend most of each workday working with crops and other plants. Typical duties include genetically engineering plants to produce more pest-resistant crops, growing more nutritious crops, and making the food derived from those crops last longer on store shelves. Agricultural biochemists also devote parts of their days to monitoring the effects of pollution on the environment.

A Clinical Biochemist at Work

"I arrive in my hospital laboratory generally about 9.10 a.m. [and] find out if any emergencies developed that affect the patients on whom I will be working. If so, they get my priority attention. I will [then] get my technical colleagues to carry out a number of mechanized analyses or, if complex or manual analysis is required, carry it out myself."

—Janusz Knepil, clinical biochemist

Quoted in Bright Knowledge, "My Job Explained: Clinical Biochemist." www.brightknowledge.org.

Education and Training

To become an independent, working biochemist in a research facility, major company, or other setting requires a PhD in biochemistry, biology, microbiology, or chemistry. Job candidates who have only a bachelor's degree or even a master's degree can expect at best to be hired for an entry-level position in a biochemistry lab. There they will assist the full-fledged biochemists but will not be able to advance further in the job until they complete their PhDs.

The road to getting a PhD in biochemistry is long and complicated and consists of a number of years of dedicated study. The process requires first getting a bachelor's degree, then acquiring a master's degree, and finally doing graduate work to obtain the coveted PhD. On the bachelor's level, the student needs to pass courses in biology, chemistry, physics, and computer science. The math and computer science courses are essential because a working biochemist must be able to accomplish sophisticated analysis of large amounts of data.

To get a master's and PhD, the student must pass courses that include advanced microbiology, genetics, toxicology, proteomics (the study of proteins), bioinformatics (using computers to analyze massive amounts of scientific data), and a number of other specialized courses that involve hands-on work in the laboratory. Students who are diligent and ambitious (and perhaps know the right people) may be able to become an intern in a working biochemistry lab and apply that experience as credit toward their PhD.

Skills and Personality

A number of varied skills and personal traits contribute to one's success as a biochemist. First, the individual should possess strong math skills, along with a firm base in knowledge of biology, chemistry, and if possible, physics. He or she should also have robust analytical skills—that is, an ability to think critically and to investigate and solve problems as accurately as possible.

Other skills a biochemist should have include the abilities to focus and concentrate on any problems at hand, proceed with great attention to detail, display strong verbal communication skills (because it is essential that the biochemist share knowledge with an array of colleagues), and have good time-management skills (because biochemists are typically expected to meet deadlines when conducting research). Perhaps surprisingly to many, members of the profession often demonstrate artistic skills, possibly because success in this field requires a certain amount of creativity and original thinking.

Above all, a biochemist needs to be curious and inquisitive because so much knowledge in both biology and chemistry is still unknown. Speaking about his chosen science, biochemist Dario Alessi of Dundee University in Scotland says, "It is incredibly complex. Generally I think we understand less than 1/10,000 of all that there is to understand in biology. We know virtually nothing about how biology is controlled and how it works."[13]

University of California at Berkeley biochemist Jennifer Doudna was also drawn to this particular scientific discipline by a powerful desire to learn how nature works. As a child, she explains, she "spent a lot of time reading. I can remember lying on my bed a lot, just kind of thinking and wondering about how things worked, especially nature and why the animals and plants in [her hometown] had evolved the way they had."[14]

Beyond that, Doudna says, there is a more elusive, mysterious quality that the best biochemists, as well as certain other scientists, tend to display. She recalls, "I remember when I was in graduate school, thinking about my adviser [and wondering] what made him a great scientist. And the thing that stood out for me was his incredible ability to pick the right problems and go after the right questions. I don't know where it comes from. It's just sort of a sense that one has."[15]

Working Conditions

In most cases, biochemists work in labs, where they conduct experiments of various kinds. When not in the lab, they tend to be in their offices, where they use computers and other equipment to analyze the results of the experiments. Both the labs and offices may be located in a university setting or in a research facility funded either by the federal government or a private company.

Most biochemists work on teams, which frequently are interdisciplinary. In other words, a biochemist might work side by side with scientists from other fields, including engineering, physics, or computer science. All members of such a team have the same goal and freely share information with their coworkers.

Employers and Pay

Among the main employers of biochemists are colleges and universities; in such cases, biochemists are expected to teach at least some classes in addition to doing research in the school's labs. The federal government also hires biochemists to do research for medical, agricultural, and military projects. Other opportunities for jobs in biochemistry can be found in the chemical, petroleum, and pharmaceutical industries, and with biotechnology companies and cosmetics manufacturers.

Because biochemists do such specialized work and must acquire such rigorous educations, they are relatively well paid. The average annual salary for a full-time biochemist was roughly $93,000 in 2019; the lowest-paid members of the profession made $49,000, and the highest-paid made about $178,000.

What Is the Future Outlook for Biochemists?

For the immediate future, the employment outlook for biochemists is very positive. The BLS and other organizations that track

The Joy of Discovery

"The truth is that no one can ever take away from me the joy of the actual discovery. No one can take away those moments in the lab when we saw something in nature that had never been seen before. That's what I love about science. You go into the lab, do an experiment, and get a little bit of knowledge about the world that unravels another piece of the mystery of nature. I love that."

—Jennifer Doudna, biochemist

Quoted in Claudia Dreifus, "'The Joy of Discovery'—An Interview with Jennifer Doudna," *New York Review of Books*, January 24, 2019. www.nybooks.com.

career growth estimate an 11 percent growth rate for the profession between 2020 and 2026 and say there will be a need for at least ten thousand more biochemists in North America between 2020 and 2030.

One reason for this high expected growth rate is that there will be an increased demand for experts in biomedical and genetic research and the development of tests to isolate and cure various diseases affecting aging baby boomers. There will also be ever-increasing demand for research in energy sources that are environmentally safe as well as clean. The fast-growing development of genetically engineered crops and livestock will also keep biochemists in high demand.

Find Out More

American Chemical Society (ACS)
www.acs.org

The ACS website offers a good deal of information about regional programs for high school and undergraduate college students, including how to apply for internships, summer jobs, field trips, and more.

American Society of Biological Chemists (ASBC)
www.asbmb.org

The ASBC's website describes the kind of education required to become a biochemist. It also contains assorted advice on approaching a career in the field and information about advocacy programs (which develop regional hubs where scientists get together and compare and discuss their research).

Biochemical Society
https://biochemistry.org

This organization raises awareness of the importance of the biological sciences. Its website features helpful information on grants, scholarships, and regional competitions for students. In addition, it tells which colleges and universities teach biochemistry.

Society for Experimental Biology (SEB)

www.sebiology.org

The SEB helps to build contacts and relationships among biologists and other scientists. Its website contains information on how to get grants to do experiments in biology, where to attend upcoming lectures in biology and biochemistry, and how to find internships and jobs in Europe and elsewhere.

Cartographer

What Does a Cartographer Do?

Cartographers collect large amounts of data about many subjects and use it to create maps of various parts of Earth's surface. Typically, such maps show any number of features, including local, national, and international borders; elevation (distance above or below sea level); water resources; streets and highways; rainfall and other weather patterns; distribution of wildlife; and in some cases much more. The maps are routinely used by surveyors, travelers, explorers, geologists, construction crews, and military organizations. Some cartographers even use their skills to make detailed maps for imaginary lands and realms that appear in complex role-playing and video games.

Cartographers also make maps for governments to help them in urban and regional planning. Maps of this kind provide information about population density. These help government officials estimate future growth trends and plan for city expansion, distribution of first responders, and public safety, including national security.

Today, many cartographers use computerized digital technology often called GIS, which stands for Geographic Information System. Much of present GIS technology is aided by cameras on

A Few Facts

Number of Jobs
Around 12,000 in 2019

Pay
An average of $65,000 per year in 2019

Educational Requirements
Minimum of a bachelor's degree

Personal Qualities
Artistic or design skills, strong computer skills, attention to detail

Work Settings
Mainly offices, although occasional field work

Future Job Outlook
Estimated growth of 15 percent through 2028

orbiting satellites. Using digital maps that cartographers create with GIS, various organizations and individuals can conduct accurate environmental, geological, and land-use studies.

The complexity and educational potential of a number of the maps that modern cartographers fashion are impressive and in a few cases staggering. According to Paulette Hasier, a cartographer with the US Library of Congress, the maps made by today's leading cartographers are not simply collections of boundary lines drawn on paper; rather, they contain entire realms of information about the planet and human culture. "There is a world of information contained on every map!" she explains.

> For many years, maps were not seen as historical documents and I think the strength of a map as a primary source is always that it is a combination of factual and cultural information. . . . With GIS you can use geospatial data, combined with these historical sources, to analyze boundaries, to spatially construct new histories and even for policy-making decisions. Therefore, I see the maps [as] the true world of big data. . . . This unexplored intellectual territory combining history and spatial analysis is what really excites me about maps.[16]

The staff at the Sonoma Ecology Center, in Eldridge, California, agrees that the best modern maps contain a level of complexity that educates viewers and at the same time makes the world a more efficient place. Cartographers' maps, they say, "are like campfires. Everyone gathers around them because they allow people to understand complex issues at a glance, and find agreement about how to help the land."[17]

A Typical Workday

Only rarely are any two days alike for working cartographers. This is because on any given day they may tackle one or several of a number of diverse activities. If the cartographer is working on a new map design, he or she may spend several hours applying handwritten images to a preliminary paper-based map. At some point the cartographer checks to make sure the features on the new map are accurate and drawn to scale. Another part of the day may be devoted to sitting at the computer to obtain digital GIS data from remote sensors on satellites and planes.

On a different day the work might consist of editing older maps by adding new roads, structures, and landmarks and removing older ones. The next day the cartographer might go out into the field and supervise a topographic survey of a parcel of land or a patch of beach or other coastal area. Still another day may find him or her using an advanced computer to do desktop publishing of the latest map.

Education and Training

In most cases, becoming a cartographer requires a bachelor's degree, including course work in various kinds of math, art, and graphic design. The degree can be in geography, land surveying, earth science, oceanography, or GIS. Some candidates may opt for doing internships before they get their degrees, in which case the internship counts as credit toward the degree. Alternatively, interns may opt to remain assistants indefinitely rather than complete their degree; but if so, their salary will remain a good deal lower than it would be with the degree.

Skills and Personality

Knowledge of geography and basic forms of math knowledge are essential to cartographers. They should also possess good analytical thinking skills, excellent written communication skills, and strong computer skills, as is the case in most sciences today. They should also have a considerable level of artistic or design talent. In the words of the late noted American cartographer Erwin Josephus Raisz,

> The good cartographer is both a scientist and an artist. He must have a thorough knowledge of his subject and model, the Earth. . . . He must have the ability to generalize intelligently and to make a right selection of the features to show. These are represented by means of lines or colors; and the effective use of lines or colors requires more than knowledge of the subject. It requires artistic judgement.[18]

Finally, also as in other sciences, cartographers should be inquisitive and ask many questions. Mamata Akella, a cartographer at the web-mapping software service CartoDB, advises,

> Ask questions, try out new things, don't be afraid to fail, ask more questions! I've been a professional web cartographer for about 9 years now. Still, to this day, I ask questions even ones that some might consider "basic." I went from [using basic tools to using advanced ones] and if I hadn't asked all the questions that I had to all of the people I have, I don't know how I would have navigated those pretty radical shifts. Also, diversify your skill set. If I could go back . . . I would learn more about web development, scripting, and databases. . . . In this age of web cartography, those skills, in addition to design thinking, are critical.[19]

Paulette Hasier agrees and adds that members of the profession should be enthusiastic about the work. "You have to love what you do," she says. "You have to have a passion for what you do. So don't go into something half-hearted, don't go into something that's just going to become a job. You really need to be passionate about it because it may take a lot out of you."[20]

Working Conditions

Although cartographers spend much of their time in offices, certain tasks require extensive fieldwork to collect data and verify results. For example, cartographers may travel to the physical locations they are mapping to better understand the topography of the region.

Employers and Pay

The employers who hire cartographers represent a mix of governmental and private groups. According to the BLS, 33 percent, or about a third, of those employers are local town or county governments. State governments hire about 6 percent of cartographers and the federal government around 5 percent. Meanwhile, private companies—most of which pursue engineering, scientific, and agricultural projects—hire a total of about 30 percent of cartographers.

The median annual wage that these governments and companies pay their mapmakers was around $65,000 in 2019. The lowest 10 percent of cartographers earned about $41,000 for a year's work and the highest 10 percent made a bit more than $102,000.

What Is the Future Outlook for Cartographers?

The employment outlook for cartographers is extremely positive. The BLS and other organizations that monitor the job market predict that the need for new cartographers will grow a whopping 15 percent from 2020 to 2028, which is a far faster growth rate than the average for all professions.

One reason given for this unusually high pace of growth is a projected rise in consumer demand for accurate, reliable maps. Government planners—on the local, state, and federal levels alike—will need more and more maps, the experts say. Also, the internet, which itself is constantly expanding—will need an increasing number of web-based map products to illustrate and support articles on a wide range of subjects. At the same time, those cartographers who create fantasy maps for a diverse range of board, role-playing, and video games will remain in high demand.

The experts do caution that the profession of cartographer is not expansive. Thus, even with that impressive growth rate of 15 percent, only about 2,000 or so new cartographers will be hired in the coming decade. That means that the competition for job openings will remain fierce. But any given would-be cartographer should not be discouraged, says noted fantasy cartographer Rhys Davies. "Anybody working in the arts needs to have a ton of flexibility and patience," he says. "You need to try a lot of different avenues and artistic directions." He adds, "be open to taking everything on that comes your way [because] one thing can lead to another thing which can lead to another thing. . . . Do whatever you do with enjoyment and commitment and people will eventually find you. Just keep getting yourself out there."[21]

Find Out More

GIS Certification Institute
www.gisci.org

The GIS Institute provides professional certification for cartographers. The website explains to students and other prospective cartographers what is involved in getting certified and how to prepare for the certification exam.

Imaging and Geospatial Information Society (ASPRS)
www.asprs.org

The website of this organization contains information on student scholarships, how students can win awards for independent projects, and how students can find online webinars relating to cartography. Students can also find basic information about careers in cartography.

National Society of Professional Surveyors (NSPS)
www.nsps.us.com

The NSPS website features information on student mapmaking competitions, as well as scholarships for students aiming to study cartography. Also included is information about which colleges and universities offer the required degrees and courses of study.

North American Cartographic Information Society (NACIS)
https://nacis.org

The NACIS website has information on the availability of student scholarships and tells how students planning to become cartographers can enter local and regional mapmaking competitions. There is also information on how to obtain grants to finance independent cartography projects.

Food Scientist

What Does a Food Scientist Do?

"Food science is the study of everything related to food and food processing,"[22] states American food scientist Rebeca Lopez-Garcia, who has worked in several foreign countries to help them avert local food-related crises. Food scientists, sometimes called agricultural scientists, conduct experiments and evaluate data they or someone else has gathered about various foods and food production methods. Their conclusions may become the basis for innovative new ways to expand agricultural output or improve the quality of society's overall food supply.

Veteran food scientist Helen Mitchell points out that her discipline "is a complex multidisciplinary subject involving a combination of sciences and a knowledge of the composition of food materials and their physical, biological and biochemical behavior." She adds that the term *food technology*, today often used in reference to food science, "is the application of food science to market, manufacture, and providing safe food products to the consumer."[23]

Most Americans take the manufacture, marketing, and distribution of food for granted because in general the United States is a rich country with plentiful resources. But not all nations

A Few Facts

Number of Jobs
About 36,000 in 2019

Pay
An average of $65,000 in 2019

Educational Requirements
Minimum of a bachelor's degree

Personal Qualities
Attention to detail, good verbal communication skills

Work Settings
Mostly labs and offices, with some traveling now and then

Future Job Outlook
Estimated growth of 7 to 9 percent through 2028

are always food secure. Hence, some food scientists travel to and assist countries experiencing food crises of one type or another. Lopez-Garcia describes what she did in several such nations:

> I have [aided] coffee producers in Ecuador so they can export their coffee without contamination problems. I helped manage a wheat contamination crisis in Uruguay and helped the country develop a national action plan to control mycotoxin contamination and avoid future crisis. I have worked with the governments of Egypt and Panama to help their food industry become more competitive. Currently, I am working with the Dominican Republic to develop a national food inspection system. I also work with many multinational companies helping them develop suppliers and improve food safety.[24]

Lopez-Garcia also argues that food scientists acquire "a great sense of purpose since nutrition is essential for good health. In addition, food and eating are very social so your work is present in everybody's family events. You can really make a difference in this area."[25]

A Typical Workday

The duties and tasks of a food scientist tend to be extremely varied. Hence, in Lopez-Garcia's words, "every day is different and very interesting." Indeed, she says, "I never ever get bored because every day I have a different challenge."[26] Typical responsibilities and individual projects a food scientist might face in a given day include conducting research and experiments to enhance the quantity and quality of various crops; doing the same for domesticated farm animals; inventing new food products; and finding new, more effective ways to process, package, and deliver food products.

When traveling and working outdoors or in foreign labs, a food scientist may spend time designing field experiments. This often requires collecting and analyzing soil, water, minerals, and other natural substances. Having analyzed them, the food scientist may spend time at the computer constructing "food models" or planning step-by-step ways to improve the amount and quality of the foods in a given region or nation.

Although specific tasks and duties can vary widely, frequently part of a food scientist's daily routine is sampling various foods he or she is working with. Phoenix, Arizona–based food scientist Adam Yee explains with a touch of humor,

> We as food scientists have to sample food every day and if you love food, it's inevitable you'll take three times the amount of food you're supposed to sample. This of course, adds up. It wouldn't be so bad, but when you have a whole team who loves food, likes to try new things, and brings you the newest holiday cookies 'for research,' calorie counting goes out the window.[27]

Education and Training

The minimum educational requirement to become a food scientist is a bachelor's degree. Most often the degree is in biology, chemistry, agricultural science, or a closely related field. Also, working food scientists encourage those young people who want to enter the profession to take courses in nutrition, engineering, product development, computer science, and business management.

Some individuals in the profession sooner or later go on to get master's or doctorate degrees. "In terms of how a PhD has helped me in my career," Mitchell says, "I would say that it has given me confidence in my own ability and has certainly 'opened doors' that would not have been available with just a bachelor's."[28]

Skills and Personality

A number of different skill, knowledge, and personality attributes are helpful for achieving success as a food scientist. These include a basic knowledge of chemistry, math, biology, manufacturing processes, the safe disposal of dangerous chemicals, and especially food production methods. As Mitchell points out,

> Key abilities for staff members working in this multidisciplinary [occupation] would include being able to demonstrate that you have some working knowledge of the food industry and effective food ingredients with a strong scientific foundation. It is always advisable to be aware of the latest nutrition and health research and to be able to demonstrate that you can distinguish between consumer fads and trends.[29]

Also, food scientists should possess the ability to pay strict attention to detail, as they are regularly exposed to complex ideas from several different scientific disciplines. In addition, a food scientist should demonstrate good analytical thinking skills to sort through all that data, and effective verbal communication skills to convey it to colleagues and clients.

Working Conditions

Most food scientists spend their workday in a lab or office, where they examine and analyze data and write detailed reports using advanced computer software. From time to time, however, they need to go out into the field—which can take the form of a farm,

Food scientists, sometimes called agricultural scientists, conduct experiments and evaluate data that is used to enhance the quality of various crops. Their conclusions may become the basis for new ways to expand agricultural output or improve the quality of society's overall food supply.

food warehouse, or food processing plant. The BLS here summarizes some of the tasks and projects—lab-, office-, and field-oriented ones alike—that food scientists may tackle:

> Food scientists in private industry commonly work for food production companies, farms, and processing plants. They may improve inspection standards or overall food quality. They spend their time in a laboratory, where they do tests and experiments, or in the field, where they take samples or assess overall conditions. Other agricultural and food scientists work for pharmaceutical companies, where they use biotechnology processes to develop drugs or other medical products. Some look for ways to process agricultural products into fuels, such as ethanol produced from corn. At universities, agricultural and food scientists do research and investigate new methods of improving animal or soil health, nutrition, and other facets of food quality. They also write grants to organizations, such as the U.S. Department of Agriculture (USDA) or the National Institutes of Health (NIH), to get funding for their research.[30]

When working in the field is necessary, says Yee, "you have to travel often, and at many points, due to moments of crisis" in a given nation. "Sometimes these trips can last one day, or a month. It depends on how vital it is."[31]

Employers and Pay

The BLS estimates that roughly 19 percent of food scientists work for food-growing or food-processing companies. Another 17 percent work in college and university settings, where they do research in local labs, monitor conditions in local food facilities, and perhaps teach a few classes. About 10 percent of food scientists work in independent research labs, and 9 percent work in government-sponsored labs. Most of the rest act as independent consultants for hire.

On average, food scientists earned about $65,000 annually in 2019. The lowest-paid 10 percent made between $37,000 and $38,000, and the highest-paid 10 percent made between $116,000 and $118,000 a year. Addressing the average salary, Yee points out, "No, you won't get paid as much as an engineer. Engineers get paid more for the specific reason that their output sells for a generally higher price than your output, or what they accomplish is either a matter of safety or luxury." With a comical flair, he adds, "In general, the courses they have to study in college are a lot harder than your classes."[32]

What Is the Future Outlook for Food Scientists?

The need for new food scientists is expected to grow by 7 to 9 percent between 2020 and 2028, which is a little faster than the average for all occupations. Thus, as Mitchell says, food scientists continue to be in demand. She goes on to say that food scientists "can make a real difference to a company's fortunes and to [a nation's] population health. The food industry is a global business so the opportunities for travel and working internationally are vast and varied."[33]

Yee also stresses the job's travel opportunities as a major plus of the profession. When asked to list the reasons someone might want to consider becoming a food scientist, he responds, "If you truly love food and want to feed the world; if you truly want to express your creativity by creating products that people can eat all around the world; if you dream to visit cities and towns and try their cuisine; then this is the profession for you."[34]

Find Out More

Crop Science Society of America (CSSA)
www.crops.org

The CSSA's website explains how to become a member. It also contains information on how to get scholarships in food science at various colleges and universities and how young people can be considered for awards for doing student projects in food science–related areas.

Institute of Food Technologies (IFT)
www.ift.org

The IFT website features information about existing career choices, along with instructions on how to become certified in food science. There is also helpful information indicating where young people can study food science.

US Department of Agriculture (USDA)
www.usda.gov

The USDA's website contains information on farming, food, nutrition, conservation, and more. For young people thinking about becoming food scientists, there is information on career opportunities and agricultural projects that they can presently pursue.

Forensic Science Technician

What Does a Forensic Science Technician Do?

Depending on the preferences of individual states, cities, or police departments, forensic science technicians are sometimes called criminalists or more simply forensic scientists. Their main task is to aid in criminal investigations by analyzing evidence in a laboratory setting. With occasional exceptions, forensic science technicians do *not* visit crime scenes and collect evidence, as happens in a number of television shows and movies. Gathering the evidence at the scene of a crime is the job of crime scene investigators (CSIs), who are sometimes called forensic evidence technicians. The latter pass the evidence on to the forensic science technicians in the lab, so these two kinds of criminal investigators work in tandem, and their jobs complement each other.

Michael Howard, a self-employed forensic scientist with close to thirty years of experience in the profession, elaborates a bit. He points out that when it comes to television portrayals of his occupation, it is often less about what a forensic science technician does and more about what he or she does not do. "On television shows like *CSI*," he says,

---

A Few Facts

Number of Jobs
About 17,000 in 2019

Pay
Average of $59,000 a year in 2019

Educational Requirements
Minimum of a bachelor's degree

Personal Qualities
Strong sense of curiosity, much attention to detail, critical thinking skills

Work Settings
Mostly labs

Future Job Outlook
Estimated growth of 14 to 17 percent through 2026

they have criminalists interviewing and arresting people. In real life criminalists do not do that. In some states we can only use the evidence that has been collected by police officers. In other states there are teams [of CSIs] that process crime scenes. The person who collects the evidence may not be the one who actually analyzes it. Each piece of evidence goes to its own specialty: DNA, firearms, drugs, toxicology, or trace evidence.[35]

A Typical Workday

The average workday of a forensic science technician varies considerably because the job entails numerous possible tasks and duties. In the words of Emily Esquivel, a forensic scientist in the police department of Beaumont, Texas, "The best part of this job is every day brings in something different!" Although she spends most of her days analyzing evidence, she explains, on occasion she testifies in court or lectures in a training seminar for law enforcement personnel. Regarding the bulk of her work hours, she says that on a typical day

> I would be in the lab doing chemical analysis on evidence from cases such as possession of illegal drugs or determining the alcohol concentration of a blood sample from a suspect accused of drinking and driving. After all analysis in a case is complete, I would spend some time writing technical reports on my findings. These reports would then be submitted to the police agency that requested the analysis.[36]

Other specific tasks that Esquivel and other forensic science technicians tackle include classifying and organizing evidence in storage facilities adjacent to the lab, ensuring that proper lab procedures are followed, and ordering new lab supplies and equipment. When called upon to inspect evidence, these technicians might handle human tissue, bodily fluids, and DNA; analyze handwriting, signatures, and ink on paper; or recover missing

The Underbelly of the Job

"A lot of what I do deals with the underbelly of society and it's not necessarily fun to do that. I encounter bad stuff: mutilated bodies, child abuse, autopsies. Sometimes people say, 'I can't do this anymore, I don't want to see any more dead bodies . . . ' In forensics we often develop a warped sense of humor; we find humor in grotesque things. Forensic folks together will laugh about stuff that would horrify people outside the field."

—Michael Howard, forensic science technician

Quoted in All Criminal Justice Schools, "A Forensic Scientist Talks About the Job." www.all criminaljusticeschools.com.

data from computers, cell phones, and other electronic devices. Sometimes they collaborate in various ways with CSIs working on a case, and when they are not occupied with case work, they might conduct periodic research to keep abreast of the newest forensic technical advances.

Overall, a forensic science technician's workday usually encompasses standard business hours. But there are exceptions. Now and then the police require answers about some piece of evidence as quickly as possible, and in such cases the technician may have to work during an evening or on a weekend.

Education and Training

A minimum of a bachelor's degree is required to become a forensic science technician in most states and police departments. Some people who desire to enter the profession go further and get a master's degree. They find that this potentially leads to two favorable outcomes. One is that it differentiates them from job applicants having only a bachelor's degree, and a person with the master's may be given a more authoritative starting position in the lab when hired. The other beneficial outcome is that an applicant with more schooling almost always makes a higher starting salary.

As for the requisite bachelor's degree, there is a certain amount of flexibility in the choice of a major. Usually as long as the degree is in one of the main natural sciences, it's acceptable to most law enforcement agencies. Thus, acceptable degree fields include various branches of biology, chemistry, and physics. Some police departments will also accept a degree in criminal justice, or even law, although a double major—something like chemistry and criminal justice—is particularly attractive to hirers.

Alternatively, would-be forensic science technicians can choose to get a bachelor's degree and a master's degree, both specifically in forensic science. Only a minority of universities presently offer that major. Among the most reputable are Pennsylvania State University, Columbia College, Texas A&M University, and the University of California at Irvine. Depending on the particular major and program applicants choose, they should make sure to take certain core courses that contain knowledge essential to the job. These include genetics, toxicology, cell biology, ballistics, statistics, calculus, and criminology, among others.

Skills and Personality

A forensic science technician should first and foremost possess a strong sense of curiosity. As Michael Howard puts it, "What I enjoy most about forensic science is the problem solving. You look at the evidence to see what it's telling you. How can you use the experts, scientific tests, and your own knowledge to answer questions and solve problems?"[37]

The job also demands that the person be detail oriented by nature. Examining the evidence collected at crime scenes requires the capacity to notice tiny details and very subtle differences. Allied to that attention to detail is the precision needed to catalog evidence in such a manner that no one can later claim that someone mishandled it. The consequences of such mistakes are nothing less than seeing criminals set free thanks to legal technicalities. Critical thinking skills are also paramount because a forensic science technician must be able to question everything in order to eliminate all other possibilities before drawing final conclusions.

Besides those technical skills, effective forensic science technicians benefit greatly from solid written and verbal communication skills. This is because they are expected to regularly create detailed written reports containing complex scientific information in layman's terms. Such written materials not only help police officers, detectives, and lawyers do their jobs. As Howard points out, "You have to take notes, write reports, and be articulate enough to explain complicated science to a jury."[38]

Working Conditions

Forensic science technicians work mostly in lab settings, in which they examine and analyze evidence collected by CSIs. The forensic scientists should ideally have good working relationships with those investigators. When not working in the lab, forensic science technicians might be in court explaining their findings to a judge and jury. Or these technicians might have reason to visit the local morgue to gather information from or discuss a case with the coroner. Only on rare occasions will technicians visit a crime scene and if so, typically they will accompany the CSIs involved in an effort to double-check for possible evidence that was not found in the initial investigation.

Employers and Pay

According to the BLS, the vast majority of forensic science technicians are employed by government-sponsored labs. Close to 60 percent work in city and town police labs, and roughly 28 percent are hired by state police labs. Another 4 percent work in hospital medical labs, and perhaps 2 percent staff independent testing labs. The remaining 6 or 7 percent are freelancers who work wherever and whenever they can.

The average yearly salary earned by forensic science technicians was about $59,000 in 2019. The lowest-paid 10 percent made somewhere around $33,000 annually, whereas the highest-paid 10 percent made between $85,000 and $86,000. Overall, evidence shows that technicians' salaries tend to be higher in urban centers—especially the larger cities—where more crimes are committed each year, than in smaller towns in rural areas where crime rates tend to be lower.

What Is the Future Outlook for Forensic Science Technicians?

The outlook for the profession in the coming years is extremely positive. The BLS and other organizations that track job trends over time predict that opportunities for forensic science technicians will grow at a rate of 14 to 17 percent between 2020 and 2026, which is considerably higher than the average growth rate for all professions.

One reason for this rosy outlook, according to the BLS, is that state and local governments and police forces are expected to hire additional forensic scientists to ensure that their growing criminal case loads will be processed sufficiently. Also, ongoing annual technological advances are likely to increase the reliability and usefulness of forensic data that police introduce as evidence in trials. Because of these trends, forensic science technicians will be needed even more than they are at present, the BLS states.

In addition to increases in the actual numbers of available jobs in the profession, the competition for those jobs is expected to continue to be strong. One major reason for this robust competition is the continuing popularity of TV shows about crime scene investigations, which each year motivates a certain proportion of high school and college students to seriously consider entering the profession. Indeed, such media-generated popularity of this kind of work, according to Esquivel, "now makes every forensic job opening highly competitive."[39]

Find Out More

American Academy of Forensic Science (AAFS)
www.aafs.org

The AAFS website features information to aid young people contemplating choosing forensic science as a career. There is also a list of employment opportunities for recent college graduates and a "young forensic scientists' forum" that answers common questions about the profession.

Association of Women in Forensic Science (AWFS)
https://awifs.org

The AWFS website contains a list of networking opportunities and support chiefly for young women—teens and college students—interested in pursuing careers in forensic science. The website also lists the locales, dates, and times of upcoming lectures and demonstrations by working forensic scientists.

Council of Forensic Science Educators (COFSE)
https://cofse.org

The COFSE educates students who are considering becoming forensic science technicians. It also offers information about a forensic science honor society that has chapters in a number of colleges and universities.

Society of Forensic Toxicologists (SOFT)
www.soft-tox.org

Full membership in SOFT is open to working professionals in the field. Associate, retired, and student memberships are also available. The website provides job listings for members and offers awards for those students who show particular aptitude for forensic toxicology.

Hydrologist

What Does a Hydrologist Do?

Hydrologists study the manner in which water flows across and through the planet's surface layer, as well as through human-made pumps; how rain and snow affect groundwater levels, rivers, and lakes; and how water in and on the ground evaporates upward into the atmosphere and then falls back down again as rain and snow. Hydrologists also examine how water affects the planetary environment in general and use that knowledge to attempt to solve ongoing problems related to the quality and availability of water. Duke University hydrologist Ana Barros elaborates:

> Hydrology is a very fundamental science that has to do with water in motion. In the more traditional sense, when you think about hydrology, you think about the water cycle. But in fact, it's a lot more general. In many cases it includes water quality [and] it's all part of the hydrologic sciences. The most important aspects of hydrology are precipitation, [evaporation], and the flow of water in soils. Climate affects the water cycle by changing the amount of water that is available

A Few Facts

Number of Jobs
About 7,000 in 2019

Pay
An average of $81,000 per year in 2019

Educational Requirements
Minimum of a bachelor's degree

Personal Qualities
Solid written communication and computer skills

Work Settings
Offices, labs, and some outdoor locales

Future Job Outlook
Estimated growth of 7 percent in the 2020s

46

in the atmosphere at any given time. It also changes the rate at which water is evaporated, the water holding capacity of the atmosphere and various storm dynamics. . . . I focus a lot on clouds and precipitation processes. I'm interested in the link between aerosols, clouds, and rainfall and how all these synergies [interactions] work together.[40]

Barros also makes the important point that hydrology is a science that is in a sense composed of pieces of several other sciences, a factor she feels makes it a challenging and fascinating field of study. Hydrology, she says, is "fundamentally interdisciplinary. You can't study hydrology without also knowing about [chemistry, climatology], thermodynamics, and mechanics. It's very demanding in terms of the breadth of knowledge you need in order to make a contribution. It's a very humbling discipline in that sense."[41]

A Typical Workday

A hydrologist's typical workday depends a good deal on where she or he works. Those hydrologists who work for individual companies or local governments spend a fair amount of time measuring the properties of rivers, streams, reservoirs, and other bodies of water. They routinely collect water and soil samples to test for certain properties, such as the pH (acidic content) or inherent pollution levels. Other common daily duties can include using computer models to forecast future water supplies, the spread of pollution, and floods; analyzing data indicating existing levels of erosion, pollution, drought, and other negative aspects of the planetary water system; determining whether hydroelectric power plants, irrigation systems, and other water-related projects may be feasible; and creating written reports or lectures relating to recent findings.

Hydrologists who work in colleges and universities do many of these same things, and in addition they often teach courses in subjects related to their work. For example, Barros has the dual role of researcher and professor at Duke. "I teach a freshman seminar that's called Engineering the Planet," she explains.

At the graduate level, I teach Physical Hydrology, Hydrometeorology, Remote Sensing, and a data stimulation class. It really depends. There are days where I'm teaching and I'll come in early, teach, talk to students and have research meetings. Then there are other days where I'll shut my office door and work on research proposals and papers. In my lab, we do a lot of modeling work but we also do a lot of fieldwork so grants are crucial. For instance, I'm trying to get some time on an airplane to fly over the Great Plains and collect water vapor profiles this summer.

To emphasize how stimulating this combination of duties can be, she adds, "It's intellectually challenging and if you like to learn about new things, there's always something new to learn."[42]

Education and Training

Applicants for jobs in hydrology require at least a bachelor's degree in order to obtain even an entry level position. In comparison, veteran and senior hydrologists almost always have a master's degree or in some cases a PhD in hydrology. In getting the initial undergraduate bachelor's degree, individuals can major in one of several scientific disciplines, among them environmental science, civil engineering, geography, environmental engineering, ecology, and earth science. After obtaining the bachelor's degree, students can move on to get a master's in hydrology. In the process, they will need to take water engineering, flood risk management, and hydrogeology, to name only a few of the graduate-level courses.

Skills and Personality

Several of the skills needed to become a hydrologist are directly related to the diverse scientific knowledge and skill sets that make up

Always Something New to Learn

"Some people are very interested in one topic but a lot of smart people could be doing research on anything. If you're smart and you work hard, you can do pretty much anything. It's so important to give yourself the opportunity to explore. I think it's great to be a faculty member because . . . [there is] a lot of flexibility. It's intellectually challenging and if you like to learn about new things, there's always something new to learn."

—Ana Barros, hydrologist

Quoted in Emma Loewe, "Interview with Hydrologist Dr. Ana Barros," *Journal of Young Investigators*, April 1, 2015. www.jyi.org.

the science of hydrology itself. Because this discipline is in certain ways a combination of four, five, or more other sciences, knowledge from those disciplines comprises some of the fundamental skills of a good hydrologist. Some solid background in both advanced math and engineering is very helpful, for instance. Some good basic knowledge of chemistry, physics, geography, and mechanics is also useful.

Personal skills that make the job easier include analytical thinking, attention to detail, computer literacy, time management, and especially strong written communication skills. University of Alabama hydrologist Grey Nearing claims that another important skill for hydrologists is "the ability to handle rejection." He makes the point that many of the projects a hydrologist promotes and pursues are often funded by grants provided through individual donors, organizations, and academic institutions. These backers tend to be extremely demanding and picky, Nearing explains. He says, "It's hard to work so much, and have your grant proposals rejected so often, without losing the sense of excitement that keeps the work interesting. Academia is hyper-competitive, which was exciting at first, but starts to be a little tedious after a few years."[43]

A hydrologist takes a sample for testing. Hydrologists examine how water affects the environment and use that knowledge to solve ongoing problems related to the quality and availability of water.

Serena Ceola, a hydrologist and professor at the University of Bologna in Italy, agrees that funding projects can be very challenging and at times the lack of proper funding brings disappointment. Nevertheless, she says, "I don't have any regrets and I would re-do the same path as I did so far." This, she points out, is because an avid passion for science is an ingrained part of her personality. To young hydrologists, she recommends,

Be passionate! Since you will spend a lot of time (days and nights) on a research project, it is fundamental that you love what you are doing. Although sometimes it is difficult and you cannot see any positive outcome, be bold and keep working on your ideas. Then, search for data to support your ideas and scientific achievements. . . . This proves that your research ideas are correct. Interact with colleagues, ask them if your ideas are reasonable and create your research network. Finally, work and collaborate with inspiring colleagues, who guide and support your research activities. I had and still have the pleasure to work with fantastic mentors![44]

Working Conditions

Hydrologists spend a lot of time in their offices and in research labs, where they conduct various water-related experiments. Still, most members of the profession also go out into the field occasionally, where they collect water and soil samples, take measurements, photos, and videos of various bodies of water, and closely observe how water moves through the environment.

Employers and Pay

According to the BLS, the largest single concentration of hydrologists—about 27 percent—work for the federal government, in such agencies as the Agricultural Department, Bureau

In the Habit of Thinking a Lot

"When I'm being creative, I just think a lot. I think about projects when I'm at the gym, walking to class, eating dinner, going to bed, etc. If I think about something long enough, understand it well enough, and keep myself active, I'll often have an interesting thought. In the 10 years that I've been in the field I've gone in and out of phases where I do this vs. where I just work on routine stuff that needs to get done."

Grey Nearing, hydrologist

Quoted in Sina Khatami, "Hallway Conversations: Grey Nearing," Hydrological Uncertainty, July 20, 2019. http://hydrouncertainty.org.

of Ocean Energy Department, Environmental Protection Agency, and Tennessee Valley Authority. State governments employ another 24 percent of hydrologists, and roughly 20 percent of them work for scientific organizations. The rest are employed by private companies (such as ConocoPhillips, Exxon Mobil, Shell, and other petroleum interests), engineering firms, and town governments (including some hospitals).

The average annual salary of a hydrologist in 2019 was about $81,000. The lowest-paid 10 percent made about $49,000 a year, and the highest-paid 10 percent earned around $124,000.

What Is the Future Outlook for Hydrologists?

Experts who track job trends and growth in the United States say that the need for new hydrologists will increase by at least 7 percent in the 2020s. That rate of growth is a little faster than the average for all occupations. As for the reasons for this positive outlook, the Bureau of Labor Statistics states,

> Demand for the services of hydrologists will stem from increases in human activities such as mining, construction, and hydraulic fracturing. Environmental concerns, especially global climate change and the possibility of sea-level rise, in addition to local concerns such as flooding and drought, are likely to increase demand for hydrologists in the future.

> Managing the nation's water resources will be critical as the population grows and increased human activity changes the natural water cycle. Population expansion into areas that were previously uninhabited may increase the risk of flooding, and new communities may encounter water availability issues. These issues will all need the understanding and knowledge that hydrologists have to find sustainable solutions.[45]

Find Out More

American Geophysical Union (AGU)

www.agu.org

The organization's website features information about the AGU Bridge Program, which seeks to advance the earth and space sciences via increased representation of students in hydrology and other scientific fields. Special attention is given to Hispanic, African American, American Indian, and Pacific Islander students.

American Geosciences Institute (AGI)

www.americangeosciences.org

AGI's outreach programs in the earth sciences reach out to students through providing classroom teachers with a wide variety of resources. The website explains how the programs stress ideas for curricula, classroom activities, virtual field trips, and much more.

American Institute of Hydrology (AIH)

www.aihydrology.org

AIH recognizes students and other young people as the future of the hydrologic sciences, including hydrology. The website provides information about what types of courses related to a career in hydrology are available at various schools of higher learning.

American Water Resources Association (AWRA)

www.awra.org

AWRA provides news and information related to US water resources. Its website has a career center that advises both members and students about forthcoming career opportunities in water management, hydrology, and other sciences related to the country's water resources.

Geneticist

A Few Facts

Number of Jobs
1,500–1,600 in 2019

Pay
Average of $95,000–$105,000 annually in 2019

Educational Requirements
Minimum of a master's degree, with a doctorate preferred

Personal Qualities
Original thinking, creativity, attention to detail

Work Settings
Mostly laboratories, classrooms, and lecture halls

Future Job Outlook
Estimated growth of 10 to 11 percent in the 2020s

What Does a Geneticist Do?

Geneticists are scientists who study genes, the microscopic cells that determine people's physical characteristics. Geneticists try to determine how genes are inherited; how they activate, or switch on; and how they mutate, or change. They also study the role that genes play in disease and health and how they are affected by various environmental factors, such as climate, temperature, and pollution. Taking into account all these elements, geneticists investigate the manner in which people, animals, and plants inherit traits and how some of those traits lead to inherited diseases.

Elaborating a bit on that general description, geneticist Louisa Flintoft, editorial director of the academic publisher Springer Nature, explains that her chosen profession is largely built around "the idea that we are in large part controlled by our genes, which have been honed over millions of years of evolution to maximize their chances of being passed on to the next generation."[46]

A Typical Workday

It is difficult to describe a typical workday for a modern geneticist. This is because "every day is different [and] that's what keeps it interesting," University of Dublin geneticist Aoife McLysaght points out. "Some days are all meetings, others lectures and lecture preparation, other days are reading and writing, others are preparing for or giving talks or public demonstrations of science."[47]

Geneticists might work in a lab one day, testing patients for hereditary markers for a variety of mutations and risks of disease. Afterward they would consult with patients about the results of such tests and determine the most effective treatment or other course of action. When not active in a lab, geneticists might review scientific literature and research in order to stay abreast of recent advances in the field, or they might look over lab and team budgets. Beyond the laboratory, they may participate in community outreach programs to connect with potential patients.

Education and Training

Of the many and varied modern scientific disciplines, genetics requires more schooling than most. Obtaining a Bachelor of Science degree represents only the beginning of a geneticist's education. Leadership positions and professorships in the field require that a person go all the way, so to speak, and get a doctorate.

According to the noted college admission and preparatory group the Princeton Review, to become a full-fledged geneticist,

> A bachelor of science [BS] either in biology or chemistry is preferred, although any physical science will do as long as it is complemented with a minor in biology. [However] there are few to no positions available with only a B.S. These jobs are typically lab assistant positions with little room for career expansion. A master's in genetics helps, but to have authority in research and development a PhD. is required. Four to six years of school after completion of an undergraduate degree is the norm. The first two years are spent taking advanced science classes, and the remainder is focused on a personal research project.[48]

Proceeding with Caution

"Humans have been playing engineer since the dawn of time. . . . I completely agree that we need to be very cautious. And the more powerful, or the more rapidly-moving the technology, the more cautious we need to be, the bigger the conversation involving lots of different disciplines, religion, ethics, government, art, and so forth. And to see what its unintended consequences might be."

—George Church, geneticist

Quoted in Scott Pelley, "A Harvard Geneticist's Goal: To Protect Humans from Viruses, Genetic Diseases, and Aging," *60 Minutes*, December 8, 2019. www.cbsnews.com.

Seattle-based geneticist Katie Peichel agrees that the training period for the science of genetics is very long and laborious, but feels that it is appropriate considering the complex nature of work itself. "It took me six years to finish my PhD," she says, "then I was a postdoctoral fellow for five years. This is about how long I thought it would take, particularly given that I am a vertebrate geneticist. Experiments just take a long time!" On just how demanding the preparation for the job can be, as well as how competitive the field is, she recalls,

> My training was very rigorous, requiring both long hours at the bench and a lot of time expanding my brain too. Getting an academic position is quite competitive. Sitting on search committees now, I realize how competitive it is! I have seen searches in which several hundred people have applied for one position; many of these people have excellent credentials. Now I realize how lucky I am to have a job![49]

A number of US colleges and universities offer majors in genetics at the master's and doctoral levels. Experts agree that among the best are Harvard University and Boston University, both in Massachusetts; Duke University in North Carolina; Vanderbilt University in Tennessee; Cornell University in New York; and Stanford University in California.

Skills and Personality

To succeed in the field of genetics, geneticists must demonstrate a fairly large number of impressive skills and personality traits. First and foremost, they must possess higher-than-average reading comprehension, partly because a lot of reading is required both in training and on the job, and also because most of the information in those readings is intellectually complex. Similarly, better-than-average writing skills are needed, as geneticists frequently must write scientific papers, reports, and clinical evaluations. Also because of the cerebral nature of the work, geneticists should be adept at solving complex problems and be able to think rationally and critically.

McLysaght mentions some other skills and traits handy for the profession, saying, "Principally, I learned how to analyze and interpret data and to examine the robustness of claims made by others. I also got practice in oral presentation. Both of these have proved to be essential (and sometimes fun!)." She adds, "Apart from the obvious technical skills, I think creativity and original thinking are the most important skills; this surprises many people who don't work in science because it is not generally perceived as a creative discipline, but the ability to see new and surprising explanations for your data and experiments requires imagination."[50]

Finally, as is true in many of the sciences, a geneticist should find the work fascinating, stimulating, and even uplifting. According to Peichel,

> To succeed in running an academic research lab, you absolutely have to be passionate about your research and love what you do. The hours are long and the tangible rewards are few and far between. But, the daily rewards

are great if you love the science and training the next generation of scientists. The days when you have a student come to your office with a good result or see a formerly shy student give a great talk at a national meeting are pretty cool.[51]

Working Conditions

Geneticists spend much of their time in the lab, doing experiments and other research-related activities. They also frequent their offices, where they may do internet-related research, send and receive emails to colleagues, and meet with colleagues, patients, or students. The latter are involved if the geneticist also teaches college courses, in which case she or he will also spend a certain amount of time in the classroom. Finally, it is not unusual for geneticists to give lectures or interviews outside the classroom.

Employers and Pay

Most geneticists work in university settings, in which they both do research in labs and teach at least one course, either in genetics or another of the biological sciences. Most other geneticists work in government-sponsored labs or in hospital settings. Only a handful of members of the profession work for private companies.

Trying to Achieve a Balance

"I usually work between sixty and seventy hours a week. But you just have to choose what is important in your life and let go of other things that are less important to you. I feel most balanced when I feel like I am in control of my decisions. So, once I remember that I am choosing to work because I enjoy it, I feel much better. I also put a big priority on making a time for myself every day . . . and this also helps me immensely."

—Katie Peichel, geneticist

Quoted in Scitable, "Geneticist Katie Peichel." www.nature.com.

The amount that geneticists earn can vary, depending on their specialty. Roughly speaking, most geneticists fall into one of three categories. One is the position of research geneticist, who might or might not teach in addition to spending time in the lab. This scientist tries to understand how living things inherit physical traits. On average, research geneticists made about $100,000 yearly in 2019.

The second category is medical geneticist. Medical geneticists work mainly in hospital settings, where they specialize in both treating patients and searching for cures for genetic diseases. Some medical geneticists made as much as $150,000 in 2019.

The third category is made up of genetic counselors, who give information and advice to patients and others who want to know about the causes and possible cures of genetic diseases. Genetic counselors made an annual salary of about $82,000 in 2019.

What Is the Future Outlook for Geneticists?

According to the BLS and other organizations that track the country's employment statistics, the overall outlook for geneticists in the near future is positive. In general, the demand for them will increase at a rate of 10 to 11 percent between 2020 and 2028, moderately higher than the rate for most jobs. Moreover, singling out genetic counselors, the BLS predicts a growth rate for them of up to 27 percent in the same time period, far higher than average.

The main reason for this overall growth is that genetic information has in recent years been of interest to and within the reach of average people. Millions of Americans have sent DNA samples to companies that test it and determine someone's ethnic heritage; this activity is expected to continue to increase in the near future. Furthermore, Flintoft says, "The practical applications of genetics already affect people's lives and are going to do so increasingly in the future. For example, advances in technology mean that it may well be feasible soon for everyone living in a developed country to have their genome sequenced [and] researchers would be able to engineer altered or entirely new organisms from scratch."[52] According to Flintoft, more geneticists will be needed to staff the new research facilities that will be built to help make these advances possible.

Find Out More

American Genetics Association (AGA)
www.theaga.org

The AGA grants special event awards each year to members to support events that encourage participation by students and other young people. These events include special workshops, short courses in basic aspects of genetics, and meetings to discuss the most recent discoveries in genetics.

Genetics Society of America (GSA)

https://genetics-gsa.org

The GSA website has links that lead to primers in genetics for those young people still deciding whether to choose this profession. Other links lead to grants to pay for learning and schooling and to professional development workshops for young geneticists once they find jobs.

Society for Conservation Biology (SCB)

https://conbio.org

The SCB website has features designed to help students in their educational journeys, including how to prepare a winning résumé, helpful advice on how to prepare and deliver presentations of personal projects, and how to win various awards the organization periodically offers students.

Astronomer

What Does an Astronomer Do?

Astronomy was one of the first scientific disciplines the ancient Greeks pursued and is therefore one of the oldest existing sciences. Today there are several branches of astronomy, each with a specific set of goals. For example, planetary astronomers focus on planets, both inside and outside our solar system (the sun's family), and solar astronomers study the sun, its structure and atmosphere, and its effects on Earth and other planets. Meanwhile, stellar astronomers investigate the other stars and their life cycles, along with the extreme outcomes of their deaths: supernovas, white dwarfs, neutron stars, and black holes. Galactic astronomers survey our galaxy, the Milky Way, along with other galaxies, and cosmologists try to determine the origin, history, and potential future of the entire universe.

Within each of these disciplines, astronomers pursue various smaller-scale goals and get involved in a fairly wide array of professional activities. As an example, stellar astronomer Cathy Imhoff, of the Space Telescope Science Institute in Baltimore, Maryland, describes some of her own goals and activities. "I do all kinds of things," she says. "One reason I like my job is that I use and program

A Few Facts

Number of Jobs
About 2,500 in 2019

Pay
Average of $107,000–$120,000 in 2019

Educational Requirements
Doctorate

Personal Qualities
Creative thinking, attention to detail, patience

Work Settings
Observatories, offices, and classrooms

Future Job Outlook
Estimated growth of 9 to 10 percent by 2028

computers [to analyze data and research].” Until its termination in the late 1990s, Imhoff used the International Ultraviolet Explorer (IUE) satellite to study very young stars. Today she continues to study them using other advanced instruments. “I've been working on trying to understand what is going on in these stars for years,” she remarks.[53]

In a similar manner, planetary astronomer and UCLA professor Brad Hansen has spent years focusing on extrasolar planets—those orbiting other stars. As he explains, he tries to learn about them by comparing them to the planets in the sun's family. He seeks to learn, he says, “how our own solar system fits into the framework of the planets discovered around other stars. I have worked on the formation of the terrestrial planets [Mercury, Venus, Earth, and Mars] and am currently working on the formation of moons in the solar system and around other stars.”[54]

A Typical Workday

When they hear the term *astronomer*, most people envision a studious-looking person quietly and patiently peering through the lens of a large telescope. That image was fairly authentic before the mid-to-late twentieth century, when large telescopes became far more complex and computerized. According to the staff of the National Optical Astronomy Observatory, in Tucson, Arizona,

> Astronomers no longer look through an eye-piece on the telescopes but instead use sophisticated digital cameras attached to a telescope and computers to gather and analyze research data. The actual time spent at a telescope collecting data for analysis is only the beginning. Most of their time is spent in an office analyzing the data, creating computer programs that allow them to more efficiently search through the data, writing research papers, and completing other administrative tasks like attending meetings. There are many variables that shape an astronomer's time, so many work flexible hours that meet their unique job environments.[55]

Astronomers' days are taken up observing and analyzing various aspects of the solar system and universe. They might spend time gathering, organizing, and evaluating immense quantities of data from external observations and then trying to document the findings of those observations. They often must confer with other astronomers to research and solve problems; they also learn from colleagues by attending conferences, seminars, and other academic events. Astronomers also devote blocks of time to writing and submitting research proposals to supervisors, universities, or governments in hopes of receiving funding to carry these projects forward.

Education and Training

"It takes a lot of studying," Cathy Imhoff says, "to be a professional astronomer." By *professional*, she means "someone who does research, publishes in the professional journals, teaches at a university, and so on."[56] First, would-be astronomers have to attend college for four years and obtain a bachelor's degree in science. Typically, they major in physics and take many advanced courses in math and astronomy.

"Then you go to graduate school," Imhoff goes on. "Most astronomy departments that can award a PhD are at fairly big universities. It usually takes around six years of graduate school. [Altogether] it takes about 10 years in school. It sounds like a lot of work, but if you like it then it doesn't matter!"[57]

Skills and Personality

An effective astronomer must have a rounded set of skills and personal traits. Although attention to detail is important for any scientist, it is particularly crucial for an astronomer. Indeed, even a tiny math or computer programming error made when observing a star or other celestial object can ruin an entire night's work.

Creative thinking and writing skills are also important. First, a creative mind has a better chance of forming theories about

The Battery Driving His Curiosity

"I was . . . a very big fan of science fiction, reading about 30 novels a year from grade 8 through 12, and so my astronomy experience as a teenager was part fact and part fantasy. Science fiction acted like my 'battery' to drive my curiosity about astronomy even further. Unlike my friends in school, I actively sought-out the inspiration and awe of the night sky."

—Sten Odenwald, NASA astronomer

Quoted in Maria Miller, "Interview with an Astronomer," HomeschoolMath.net. www.home schoolmath.net.

the workings of the universe. Also, astronomers frequently have to pen reports good enough for publication, as well as submit technical papers to astronomical and other scientific journals. In a similar manner, an astronomer needs to be able to verbally communicate her or his ideas to fellow scientists or students who attend that astronomer's lectures. Overall, Imhoff states, every astronomer "must be able to write effectively, read tons of technical papers, present reports, give speeches, and communicate with other scientists from all over the world."[58]

Other skills and traits that benefit astronomers are open-mindedness and a willingness to revise or even discard older theories in the face of new evidence. They should also have a good deal of patience because proving theories can take a long time—many years in some cases. Proficiency in several technical areas, including multimillion-dollar telescopes, advanced computer software programs, and complex orbiting satellites is also desirable. In addition, NASA astronomer Sten Odenwald points out, strong math skills are a must for all astronomers. "You cannot do very much in physical science," he says, "without being fluent in mathematics because 100% of the data is numbers and 100% of the interpretation of that data uses equations and other tools in mathematics to look for patterns and relationships. On a typical

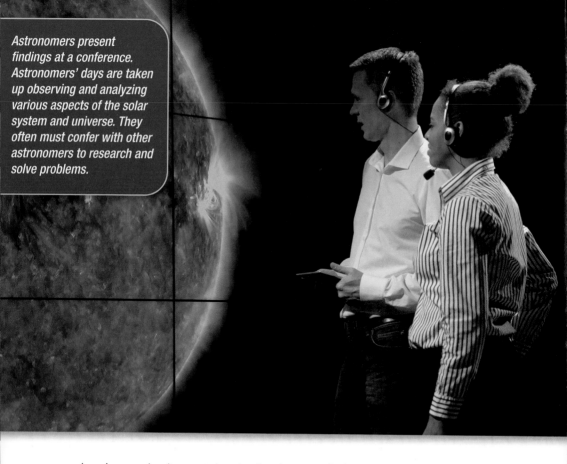

day, I use algebra and calculus in my work, so you have to be absolutely fluent in understanding how to 'speak' this language."[59] Finally, Odenwald emphasizes, astronomers must be energetic and ambitious in the pursuit of knowledge about the universe. "Don't just sit in a chair and passively expect the knowledge to 'appear' in your brain," he says. "You have to be resourceful and go after information and absorb it. Don't wait for a teacher to assign it as homework!"[60]

Working Conditions

Most astronomers work at a college or university, where they both do astronomical research and teach classes. (Frequently they teach physics as well as astronomy.) They will sometimes spend time in observatories and computer labs, but more often they will be found in their offices or classrooms. A minority of astronomers spend all of their time in observatories, either around the telescopes and computers or in their observatory-based offices. It is not uncommon for astronomers, particularly the ones who work full-time at observatories, to work several nights per week. This is because so much of the new research relies on observing and photographing the night skies.

Employers and Pay

A majority of professional astronomers are employed by colleges and universities and draw faculty pay. Most of the rest work for national observatories or federal government labs and facilities (for instance those astronomers who work at NASA). However, a small proportion of American astronomers work in the private sector, including aerospace firms, companies that work as consultants to the federal government, and privately run planetariums and science museums.

Full-time astronomers working in university settings or observatories made an average yearly salary of $107,000–$120,000 in 2019. The lowest-paid 10 percent of all astronomers made around $58,000 that year and the highest-earning 10 percent made $166,000 or more.

What Is the Future Outlook for Astronomers?

The demand for new astronomers is expected to grow by a rate of 9 to 10 percent between 2020 and 2028. That is somewhat faster than the growth rate for most jobs in the country. Although that is a positive outlook, it is important to point out that astronomy is a relatively small scientific discipline, with only between two and three thousand positions in the whole country. Thus, at any given time, there are only a couple hundred job openings at best.

This means that young people who are motivated to become astronomers should be realistic about their future prospects. If they work hard and make good grades in college, they may achieve their dream of becoming an astronomer. But because the field is so competitive, they may ultimately need to either take

The Hardest Thing About the Job

"I think that the hardest part for me and for most astronomers is having to keep asking for money so we can do research. In order to get the money to visit observatories, pay students to help reduce the data, publish papers, buy and use computers, etc. astronomers frequently have to write proposals. . . . It is no fun, and it takes away from our time to actually do the science!"

—Cathy Imhoff, astronomer

Quoted in Scholastic, "Career as an Astronomer: Cathy Imhoff." www.scholastic.com.

many years to land a choice job, or settle for a field that is only loosely related to astronomy. The staff of the National Optical Astronomy Observatory advises:

> Because astronomy is a relatively small field but attractive to many students, there is great competition for jobs. After attaining a PhD, it is common to take a postdoctoral position [a sort of part-time or assistant astronomer]. . . . For individuals who like the field of astronomy, but don't want to be an astronomer [or cannot find steady work as one], there are telescope operator technicians . . . administrators . . . educators, and [other tangential positions]. Most observatories, laboratories, colleges, and universities have employment pages to search through for jobs that may fit your skill set.[61]

Find Out More

American Astronomical Society (AAS)
http://aas.org

The website of the AAS features a generous section about education and public outreach. The AAS has a program called Astronomy Ambassadors, which organizes workshops to teach would-be astronomers how to develop their skills and communicate more clearly.

International Astronomical Union (IAU)

www.iau.org

The IAU, which serves as the authority for naming celestial bodies and their features, includes in its website information about its Office for Young Astronomers. Among other services, it pays travel and transportation expenses to students who want to attend lectures by professional astronomers.

National Aeronautics and Space Administration (NASA)

www.nasa.gov

The website of the official US space agency, NASA, contains a section on opportunities for students and other young people. It includes information about both NASA internships and fellowships and how students can begin to seriously explore eventually having a career at NASA.

Planetary Society

www.planetary.org

The organization's website features a section on how students and ordinary citizens can attend Planetary Society functions and lectures and be on its mailing list. There is also information about a program in which young people can submit student projects to the society and receive recognition for them.

Source Notes

Why Become a Scientist?

1. Quoted in Polymer Solutions Incorporated, "Why Should Someone Want to Be a Scientist?" March 21, 2016. www.polymersolutions.com.
2. Quoted in Polymer Solutions Incorporated, "Why Should Someone Want to Be a Scientist?"
3. Dick Ahlstrom, "Ten Great Reasons to Become a Scientist," *Irish Times*, March 10, 2016. www.irishtimes.com.
4. Quoted in Autumn Spanne, "10 Facts About Being a Climate Scientist—From Climate Scientists," Mental Floss, March 17, 2017. www.mentalfloss.com.
5. Quoted in American Scientist, "75 Reasons to Become a Scientist." www.americanscientist.org.

Climate Scientist

6. Quoted in Spanne, "10 Facts About Being a Climate Scientist—From Climate Scientists."
7. Quoted in Brian Kahn, "This Is What It's Like to Be a Young Climate Scientist," Climate Central, October 19, 2016. www.climatecentral.org.
8. Quoted in Science Learning Hub, "Dr. Mike Williams," March 1, 2017. www.sciencelearn.org.nz.
9. Spanne, "10 Facts About Being a Climate Scientist—From Climate Scientists."
10. Quoted in Jem Bendell, "Climate Scientist Speaks About Letting Down Humanity and What to Do About It," *Professor Jem Bendell*, July 31, 2019. https://jembendell.com.
11. Quoted in Kahn, "This Is What It's Like to Be a Young Climate Scientist."

Biochemist

12. Quoted in Bright Knowledge, "My Job Explained: Clinical Biochemist." www.brightknowledge.org.

13. Quoted in Tomorrow Edition, "Interview with Biochemist and LRRK2 Expert Prof. Dario Alessi," September 18, 2018. https://tmrwedition.com.
14. Quoted in Claudia Dreifus, "'The Joy of Discovery'—An Interview with Jennifer Doudna," *New York Review of Books*, January 24, 2019. www.nybooks.com.
15. Quoted in Dreifus, "'The Joy of Discovery'—An Interview with Jennifer Doudna."

Cartographer

16. Quoted in John Hessler, "Rising to the First: An Interview with Dr. Paulette Hasier," Library of Congress, March 22, 2019. https://blogs.loc.gov.
17. Quoted in Caitlyn Dempsey, "GIS and Cartography Quotes," GIS Lounge, November 14, 2018. www.gislounge.com.
18. Quoted in Dempsey, "GIS and Cartography Quotes."
19. Quoted in Muthukumar Kumar, "How Does It Feel to Be a Cartographer in the Age of Google Maps? Interview with Mamata Akella," Geoawesomeness, March 22, 2016. https://geoawesomeness.com.
20. Quoted in Hessler, "Rising to the First: An Interview with Dr. Paulette Hasier."
21. Quoted in Dream Foundry, "Interview with Freelance Cartographer Rhys Davies," September 12, 2019. https://dreamfoundry.org.

Food Scientist

22. Quoted in EduKUDU Content Team, "An Interview with a Food Scientist." https://i-studentglobal.com.
23. Quoted in Julie Mal, "Life of a Food Scientist: Interview with Helen Mitchell," *Food Crumbles*, January 3, 2020. https://foodcrumbles.com.
24. Quoted in EduKUDU Content Team, "An Interview with a Food Scientist."
25. Quoted in EduKUDU Content Team, "An Interview with a Food Scientist."
26. Quoted in EduKUDU Content Team, "An Interview with a Food Scientist."

27. Adam Yee, "Why You Shouldn't Be a Food Scientist," My Food Job Rocks!" https://myfoodjobrocks.com.
28. Quoted in Mal, "Life of a Food Scientist: Interview with Helen Mitchell."
29. Quoted in Mal, "Life of a Food Scientist: Interview with Helen Mitchell."
30. US Bureau of Labor Statistics, "What Agricultural and Food Scientists Do," September 4, 2019. www.bls.gov.
31. Yee, "Why You Shouldn't Be a Food Scientist."
32. Yee, "Why You Shouldn't Be a Food Scientist."
33. Quoted in Mal, "Life of a Food Scientist: Interview with Helen Mitchell."
34. Yee, "Why You Shouldn't Be a Food Scientist."

Forensic Science Technician

35. Quoted in All Criminal Justice Schools, "A Forensic Scientist Talks About the Job." www.allcriminaljusticeschools.com.
36. Quoted in Scientific Minds, "I Heart My Science Career! An Interview with a Forensic Scientist," August 3, 2016. www .scientificminds.com.
37. Quoted in All Criminal Justice Schools, "A Forensic Scientist Talks About the Job."
38. Quoted in All Criminal Justice Schools, "A Forensic Scientist Talks About the Job."
39. Quoted in Scientific Minds, "I Heart My Science Career! An Interview with a Forensic Scientist."

Hydrologist

40. Quoted in Emma Loewe, "Interview with Hydrologist Dr. Ana Barros," *Journal of Young Investigators*, April 1, 2015. www .jyi.org.
41. Quoted in Loewe, "Interview with Hydrologist Dr. Ana Barros."
42. Quoted in Loewe, "Interview with Hydrologist Dr. Ana Barros."
43. Quoted in Sina Khatami, "Hallway Conversations: Grey Nearing," Hydrological Uncertainty, July 20, 2019. http://hydro uncertainty.org.
44. Quoted in European Geosciences Union, "YHS Interview Serena Ceola: Shedding Light on Interrelations Between Hu-

man Impacts and River Networks," October 9, 2019. https://
blogs.egu.eu.

45. US Bureau of Labor Statistics, "Hydrologists: Job Outlook,"
September 4, 2019. www.bls.gov.

Geneticist

46. Quoted in Bio-Med Central, "Ask a Geneticist: A Q+A with
Louisa Flintoft," April 22, 2016. https://blogs.biomedcentral
.com.
47. Quoted in EduKUDU, "An Interview with a Genetic Scientist."
https://i-studentglobal.com.
48. Princeton Review, "Geneticist." www.princetonreview.com.
49. Quoted in Scitable, "Geneticist Katie Peichel." www.nature
.com.
50. Quoted in EduKUDU, "An Interview with a Genetic Scientist."
51. Quoted in Scitable, "Geneticist Katie Peichel."
52. Quoted in Bio-Med Central, "Ask a Geneticist: A Q+A with
Louisa Flintoft."

Astronomer

53. Quoted in Scholastic, "Career as an Astronomer: Cathy Imhoff." www.scholastic.com.
54. "Brad Hansen" [faculty description], UCLA Division of Astronomy and Astrophysics. www.astro.ucla.edu.
55. National Optical Astronomy Observatory, "Astronomy Is the
Study of the Universe: Everything About Stars and Planets,
Galaxies, Dark Matter, and Energy." www.noao.edu.
56. Quoted in Scholastic, "Career as an Astronomer: Cathy Imhoff."
57. Quoted in Scholastic, "Career as an Astronomer: Cathy Imhoff."
58. Quoted in Scholastic, "Career as an Astronomer: Cathy Imhoff."
59. Quoted in Maria Miller, "Interview with an Astronomer," Home-
schoolMath.net. www.homeschoolmath.net.
60. Quoted in Miller, "Interview with an Astronomer."
61. National Optical Astronomy Observatory, "Astronomy Is the
Study of the Universe: Everything About Stars and Planets,
Galaxies, Dark Matter, and Energy."

Interview with a Biochemist

John Stegeman is a distinguished senior scientist in the biology department of the renowned Woods Hole Oceanographic Institute in southeastern Massachusetts. As a biochemist, his interests include the effects of pollutants on human and animal metabolism and the metabolism of marine animals.

Q: Why did you become a biochemist?
A: The lure of biochemistry is like the lure of science of any kind. Curiosity is one essential element. How do things work? What is the world made of? How did we get here? There is a desire to solve puzzles and to understand nature, from the smallest atomic level to the structure and evolution of the universe.

For the biochemist, there is a drive to understand how proteins work, how they are made, what they do. For me, it was how enzymes work, and what they do. And there is deep desire to know what controls all of these things in the cell, and how different cells, for example in the liver, the heart and the brain, differ in this regard. Do things work the same or differently in different species, from worms to whales? The fascination with learning something new about nature, about solving the puzzle draws you into the research and at its best, each day is another day when you might solve the puzzle you have been working on.

These things led me to be a biochemist. It started and the puzzles kept drawing me forward.

Q: Can you describe your typical workday?
A: The workday of a biochemist can vary depending on what is required at the moment, and on a person's role in a laboratory. For the research team leader, the day begins with communicating with colleagues with whom you have been working. These people may

be in the next room, or on opposite sides of the world. Research today is largely an international collaboration.

The work itself sometimes involves writing papers to publish what you have found, or writing grant applications for funding that you need to do the research. Then there will be discussions with people in the laboratory about some specific aspects of the studies you have going on at the moment—what are the next experiments to do? And there will be writing, of the papers or proposals. While that sounds dull, it often is exciting, as putting the findings into words often triggers a new thought and a new understanding.

Q: What do you like most about your job?
A: There is an excitement in being able to ask questions about how things work, and figure out how to answer those questions. And when you do, you will learn something that likely no one else on Earth knows at that time, until you publish the results. There also is the possibility that what you learn may benefit others, in biomedical or environmental sciences.

And a most appealing aspect is making close friends from places around the world, friends who do similar work, friends with whom you collaborate, and who you see at international meetings. It is an enriching part of being a scientist generally.

Q: What do you like least about your job?
A: Well, while writing proposals can be exciting, with a group discussion of something entirely new, if they do not get funded—if you do not succeed in raising the money—then you may not be able to go after the questions. And sometimes, it means you have to tell someone that without the funding, they may have to seek another position.

Q: What personal qualities do you find most valuable for this type of work?
A: Having a driving curiosity is as I said, very important. The ability to be self-driven is also important. That varies depending on what

type of job you have in biochemistry, whether it is in academic research or in a company. Being absolutely honest about what results you find. Being a good team player. Sometimes being able to work alone for long periods.

Q: What advice do you have for students who might be interested in this career?
A: Learn as much as you can. Do not be put off by the idea of memorizing things—pack your brain with as much as you can, so that new ideas can come from the wealth of things you learn. Take math courses too. Good writing is very important.

It can be a fascinating career, and a true luxury, to have a job in which you get to ask questions, and figure out how to answer them. Being paid to think, and act on those thoughts, to think about nature and how it works, that is wonderful.

Other Jobs in Science

Agricultural technician
Anthropologist
Archaeologist
Bacteriologist
Biologist
Botanist
Chemist
Civil engineer
Dendrologist
Dermatologist
Ecologist
Embryologist
Entomologist
Ethologist
Geological technician
Geologist
Immunologist
Mathematician
Mechanical engineer
Meteorologist

Microbiologist
Mineralogist
Neurologist
Nurse practitioner
Oceanographer
Ornithologist
Paleontologist
Pathologist
Physician
Political scientist
Psychologist
Radiologist
Seismologist
Software applications developer
Statistician
Surveyor
Toxicologist
Urologist
Web developer
Zoologist

Editor's note: The online *Occupational Outlook Handbook* of the US Department of Labor's Bureau of Labor Statistics is an excellent source of information on jobs in hundreds of career fields, including many of those listed here. The *Occupational Outlook Handbook* may be accessed online at www.bls.gov/ooh.

Index